OLD AND NEW

OLD AND NEW

poems to enjoy

selected by
James Gibson
and
Raymond Wilson

illustrated by
Chris Gilbert

John Murray

© James Gibson and Raymond Wilson 1986

First published 1986 by John Murray (Publishers) Ltd,
50 Albemarle Street, London W1X 4BD

Typeset by Latimer Trend & Company Ltd, Plymouth
Printed in Great Britain by Martin's of Berwick

British Library Cataloguing in Publication Data

Old and new: poems to enjoy.
  1. English poetry—19th century 2. English
poetry—20th century
I. Gibson, James, 1919–   II. Wilson, Raymond, 1925–
821'.008'09282   PR1221

ISBN 0–7195–4241–3

Contents

Story Poems

Word Pictures

Song and Dance

Poems for Fun

⊱ STORY POEMS ⊰

from **Beowulf**

Traditional

(Translated by Ian Serraillier)

        Over the misty moor
From the dark and dripping caves of his grim lair,
Grendel with fierce ravenous stride came stepping.
A shadow under the pale moon he moved,
That fiend from hell, foul enemy of God,
Toward Heorot. He beheld it from afar, the gleaming
      roof
Towering high to heaven. His tremendous hands
Struck the studded door, wrenched it from the hinges
Till the wood splintered and the bolts burst apart.
Angrily he prowled over the polished floor,
A terrible light in his eyes—a torch flaming!
As he scanned the warriors, deep-drugged in sleep,
Loud loud he laughed, and pouncing on the nearest
Tore him limb from limb and swallowed him whole,
Sucking the blood in streams, crunching the bones.
Half-gorged, his gross appetite still unslaked,
Greedily he reached his hand for the next—little
      reckoning
For Beowulf. The youth clutched it and firmly
      grappled.

Such torture as this the fiend had never known.
In mortal fear, he was minded to flee to his lair,
But Beowulf prisoned him fast. Spilling the benches,
They tugged and heaved, from wall to wall they hurtled.
And the roof rang to their shouting, the huge hall
Rocked, the strong foundations groaned and trembled.
Then Grendel wailed from his wound, his shriek of pain
Roused the Danes in their hiding and shivered to the
      stars.
The warriors in the hall spun reeling from their
      couches,
In dull stupor they fumbled for their swords, forgetting
No man-made weapon might avail. Alone, Beowulf
Tore Grendel's arm from his shoulder asunder,
Wrenched it from the root while the tough sinews
      cracked.
And the monster roared in anguish, well knowing
That deadly was the wound and his mortal days ended.
Wildly lamenting, away into the darkness he limped,
Over the misty moor to his gloomy home.
But the hero rejoiced in his triumph and wildly waved
In the air his blood-soaked trophy.

        And the sun,
God's beacon of brightness, banishing night,
Made glad the sky of morning. From near and far
The Danes came flocking to Heorot to behold
The grisly trophy—Grendel's giant arm
Nailed to the wall, the fingertips outspread,
With nails of sharpened steel and murderous spikes
Clawing the roof. Having drunk their fill of wonder,
Eagerly they followed his track to the lake, and there
Spellbound they stared at the water welling with blood,
Still smoking hot where down to the joyless deep
He had dived, downward to death. And they praised
      Beowulf
And swore that of all men under the sun, beyond
      measure
Mightiest was he and fittest to govern his people.

from Reynard the Fox

John Masefield

The fox was strong, he was full of running,
He could run for an hour and then be cunning,
But the cry behind him made him chill,
They were nearer now and they meant to kill.
They meant to run him until his blood
Clogged on his heart as his brush with mud,
Till his back bent up and his tongue hung flagging,
And his belly and brush were filthed from dragging.

The pure clean air came sweet to his lungs,
Till he thought foul scorn of those crying tongues.
In a three mile more he would reach the haven
In the Wan Dyke croaked on by the raven.
In a three-mile more he would reach the haven
On the hard cool floor of a Wan Dyke earth,
Too deep for spade, too curved for terrier,
With the pride of the race to make rest the merrier.
In a three-mile more he would reach his dream,
So his game heart gulped and he put on steam.

Like a rocket shot to a ship ashore
The lean red bolt of his body tore,
Like a ripple of wind running swift on grass;
Like a shadow on wheat when a cloud blows past,
Like a turn at the buoy in a cutter sailing
When the bright green gleam lips white at the railing,
Like the April snake whipping back to sheath,
Like the gannets' hurtle on fish beneath,
Like a kestrel chasing, like a sickle reaping,
Like all things swooping, like all things sweeping,
Like a hound for stay, like a stag for swift,
With his shadow beside like spinning drift.

In one mile more he would lie at rest,
So for one mile more he would go his best.
He reached the dip at the long droop's end
And he took what speed he had still to spend.

As he raced the corn towards Wan Dyke Brook
The pack had view of the way he took;
Robin hallooed from the downland's crest,
He capped them on till they did their best.
The quarter-mile to the Wan Brook's brink
Was raced as quick as a man can think.

And here, as he ran to the huntsman's yelling,
The fox first felt that the pace was telling;
His body and lungs seemed all grown old,
His legs less certain, his heart less bold,
The hound-noise nearer, the hill-slope steeper,
The thud in the blood of his body deeper.
His pride in his speed, his joy in the race
Were withered away, for what use was pace?
He had run his best, and the hounds ran better,
Then the going worsened, the earth was wetter.
Then his brush drooped down till it sometimes dragged,
And his fur felt sick and his chest was tagged
With taggles of mud, and his pads seemed lead,
It was well for him he'd an earth ahead.

Down he went to the brook and over,
Out of the corn and into the clover,
Over the slope that the Wan Brook drains,
Past Battle Tump where they earthed the Danes,
Then up the hill that the Wan Dyke rings
Where the Sarsen Stones stand grand like kings.

He passed the Sarsens, he left the spur,
He pressed uphill to the blasted fir,
He slipped as he leaped the hedge; he slithered.
'He's mine,' thought Robin. 'He's done, he's dithered.'

At the second attempt he cleared the fence,
He turned half-right where the gorse was dense,
He was leading the hounds by a furlong clear.
He was past his best, but his earth was near.
He ran up gorse to the spring of the ramp,
The steep green wall of the dead men's camp,
He sidled up it and scampered down
To the deep green ditch of the Dead Men's Town.

Within, as he reached that soft green turf,
The wind, blowing lonely, moaned like surf,
Desolate ramparts rose up steep
On either side, for the ghosts to keep.

He raced the trench, past the rabbit warren,
Close-grown with moss which the wind made barren;
He passed the spring where the rushes spread,
And there in the stones was his earth ahead:
One last short burst upon failing feet—
There life lay waiting, so sweet, so sweet,
Rest in a darkness, balm for aches.
The earth was stopped. It was barred with stakes.

The Forest Fire

Sir C. G. D. Roberts

The night was grim and still with dread,
No star shone down from heaven's dome;
The ancient forest closed around
    The settler's lonely home.

There came a glare that lit the north;
There came a sound that roused the night;
But child and father slumbered on,
    Nor felt the growing light.

There came a noise of flying feet,
With many a strange and dreadful cry;
And sharp flames crept and leapt along
    The red verge of the sky.

There came a deep and gathering roar,
The father raised his anxious head;
He saw the light like a dawn of blood
    That streamed across his bed.

It lit the old clock on the wall,
It lit the room with splendour wild,
It lit the fair and tumbled hair
    Of the still sleeping child.

And zig-zag fence, and rude log barn,
And chip-strewn yard, and cabin grey,
Glowed crimson in the reddening glare
    Of that untimely day.

The boy was hurried from his sleep;
The horse was hurried from his stall;
Up from the pasture clearing came
    The cattle's frightened call.

The boy was snatched to the saddle bow,
Wildly, wildly, the father rode,
Behind them swooped the hordes of flame
    And harried their abode.

The scorching heat was at their heels;
The huge roar hounded them on their flight;
Red smoke and many a flying brand
       Flew o'er them through the night.

And past them fled the wild-wood forms—
Far-striding moose, and leaping deer,
And bounding panther, and coursing wolf,
       Terrible-eyed with fear.

And closer drew the fiery death;
Madly, madly, the father rode;
The horse began to heave and fall
       Beneath the double load.

The father's mouth was white and stern,
But his eyes grew tender with long farewell.
He said: 'Hold fast to your seat, sweetheart,
       And ride old Jerry well!

'I must go back. Ride on to the river,
Over the ford and the long marsh ride,
Straight on to the town, and I'll meet you, sweetheart,
       Somewhere on the other side.'

He slipped from the saddle, the boy rode on,
His hand clung fast in the horse's mane;
His hair blew over the horse's neck;
       His small throat sobbed with pain.

'Father! Father!' he cried aloud.
The howl of the fire-wind answered him
With the hiss of roaring flames, and crack
       Of shattering limb on limb.

But still the good horse galloped on,
With sinew braced and strength renewed.
The boy came safe to the river ford,
       And out of the deadly wood.

And now with his kinsfolk, fenced from fear,
At play in the heart of the city's hum,
He stops in his play to wonder why
       His father does not come!

The Griesly[1] Wife

John Manifold

'Lie still, my newly married wife,
    Lie easy as you can.
You're young and ill-accustomed yet
    To sleeping with a man.'

The snow lay thick, the moon was full
    And shone across the floor.
The young wife went with never a word
    Barefooted to the door.

He up and followed sure and fast,
    The moon shone clear and white.
But before his coat was on his back
    His wife was out of sight.

He trod the trail wherever it turned
    By many a mound and scree,
And still the barefoot track led on
    And an angry man was he.

He followed fast, he followed slow,
    And still he called her name,
But only the dingoes[2] of the hills
    Yowled back at him again.

His hair stood up along his neck,
    His angry mind was gone,
For the track of the two bare feet gave out
    And a four-foot track went on.

Her nightgown lay upon the snow
    As it might upon the sheet,
But the track that led on from where it lay
    Was never of human feet.

His heart turned over in his chest,
    He looked from side to side,
And he thought more of his gumwood fire
    Than he did of his griesly bride.

---

1 Gruesome, horrific. 2 Wild Australian dogs.

And first he started walking back
    And then began to run
And his quarry wheeled at the end of her track
    And hunted him in turn.

Oh, long the fire may burn for him
    And open stand the door,
And long the bed may wait empty:
    He'll not be back any more.

The Highwayman

Alfred Noyes

I

The wind was a torrent of darkness among the gusty
    trees,
The moon was a ghostly galleon tossed upon cloudy
    seas,
The road was a ribbon of moonlight over the purple
    moor,
And the highwayman came riding—
      Riding—riding—
The highwayman came riding, up to the old inn-door.

He'd a French cocked-hat on his forehead, a bunch of
    lace at his chin,
A coat of the claret velvet, and breeches of brown
    doe-skin;
They fitted with never a wrinkle: his boots were up to
    the thigh!
And he rode with a jewelled twinkle,
      His pistol butts a-twinkle,
His rapier hilt a-twinkle, under the jewelled sky.

Over the cobbles he clattered and clashed in the dark
    inn-yard,
And he tapped with his whip on the shutters, but all
    was locked and barred;

He whistled a tune to the window, and who should be
    waiting there
But the landlord's black-eyed daughter,
        Bess, the landlord's daughter,
Plaiting a dark red love-knot into her long black hair.

And dark in the dark old inn-yard a stable-wicket
    creaked
Where Tim the ostler listened; his face was white and
    peaked;
His eyes were hollows of madness, his hair like mouldy
    hay,
But he loved the landlord's daughter,
        The landlord's red-lipped daughter;—
Dumb as a dog he listened, and he heard the robber
    say—

'One kiss, my bonny sweetheart, I'm after a prize
    to-night,
But I shall be back with the yellow gold before the
    morning light;
Yet, if they press me sharply, and harry me through the
    day,
Then look for me by moonlight,
        Watch for me by moonlight,
I'll come to thee by moonlight, though hell should bar
    the way.'

He rose upright in the stirrups; he scarce could reach
    her hand,
But she loosened her hair i' the casement! His face
    burnt like a brand
As the black cascade of perfume came tumbling over his
    breast;
And he kissed its waves in the moonlight
        (Oh, sweet black waves in the moonlight!)
Then he tugged at his rein in the moonlight, and
    galloped away to the West.

He did not come in the dawning; he did not come at
     noon;
And out o' the tawny sunset, before the rise o' the
     moon,
When the road was a gipsy's ribbon, looping the purple
     moor,
A red-coat troop came marching—
        Marching—marching—
King George's men came marching, up to the old
     inn-door.

They said no word to the landlord, they drank his ale
     instead,
But they gagged his daughter and bound her to the foot
     of her narrow bed;
Two of them knelt at her casement, with muskets at
     their side!
There was death at every window;
        And hell at one dark window;
For Bess could see, through her casement, the road that
     he would ride.

They had tied her up to attention, with many a
     sniggering jest;
They had bound a musket beside her, with the barrel
     beneath her breast!
'Now keep good watch!' and they kissed her.
She heard the dead man say—
Look for me by moonlight;
       Watch for me by moonlight;
I'll come to thee by moonlight, though hell should bar the
     way!

She twisted her hands behind her; but all the knots held
     good!
She writhed her hands till her fingers were wet with
     sweat or blood!

They stretched and strained in the darkness, and the
    hours crawled by like years,
Till, now, on the stroke of midnight,
        Cold, on the stroke of midnight,
The tip of one finger touched it! The trigger at least was hers!

The tip of one finger touched it; she strove no more for
    the rest!
Up, she stood to attention, with the barrel beneath her
    breast,
She would not risk their hearing; she would not strive
    again;
For the road lay bare in the moonlight;
        Blank and bare in the moonlight;
And the blood of her veins in the moonlight throbbed to
    her love's refrain.

Tlot-tlot; tlot-tlot! Had they heard it? The horse-hoofs
    ringing clear;
Tlot-tlot, tlot-tlot, in the distance? Were they deaf that
    they did not hear?
Down the ribbon of moonlight, over the brow of the
    hill,
The highwayman came riding,
        Riding, riding!
The red-coats looked to their priming! She stood up,
    straight and still!

Tlot-tlot, in the frosty silence! *tlot-tlot,* in the echoing
    night!
Nearer he came and nearer! Her face was like a light!
Her eyes grew wide for a moment; she drew one last
    deep breath,
Then her finger moved in the moonlight,
        Her musket shattered the moonlight,
Shattered her breast in the moonlight and warned
    him—with her death.

He turned; he spurred to the Westward; he did not
    know who stood

Bowed, with her head o'er the musket, drenched with
    her own red blood!
Not till the dawn he heard it, and slowly blanched to
    hear
How Bess, the landlord's daughter,
        The landlord's black-eyed daughter,
Had watched for her love in the moonlight, and died in
    the darkness there.

Back he spurred like a madman, shrieking a curse to the
    sky,
With the white road smoking behind him and his rapier
    brandished high!
Blood-red were his spurs i' the golden noon; wine-red
    was his velvet coat;
When they shot him down on the highway,
        Down like a dog on the highway,
And he lay in his blood on the highway, with the bunch
    of lace at his throat.

And still of a winter's night, they say, when the wind is in
    the trees,
When the moon is a ghostly galleon tossed upon cloudy
    seas,
When the road is a ribbon of moonlight over the purple
    moor,
A highwayman comes riding—
        Riding—riding—
A highwayman comes riding, up to the old inn-door.

Over the cobbles he clatters and clangs in the dark
    inn-yard,
And he taps with his whip on the shutters, but all is locked
    and barred;
He whistles a tune to the window, and who should be
    waiting there
But the landlord's black-eyed daughter,
        Bess, the landlord's daughter,
Plaiting a dark red love-knot into her long black hair.

The Whale

Traditional

O, 'twas in the year of ninety four,
And of June the second day,
That our gallant ship her anchor weighed
And from Stromness bore away, brave boys!
    And from Stromness bore away!

Now Speedicut was our captain's name,
And our ship the *Lion* bold,
And we were bound to far Greenland,
To the land of ice and cold—brave boys,
    To the land of ice and cold.

And when we came to far Greenland,
And to Greenland cold came we,
Where there's ice, and there's snow, and the whalefishes
    blow,
We found all open sea—brave boys,
    We found all open sea.

Then the mate he climbed to the crow's nest high,
With his spy-glass in his hand,
'There's a whale, there's a whale, there's a whalefish,'
    he cried,
'And she blows at every span'—brave boys,
    She blows at every span.

Our captain stood on his quarter-deck,
And a fine little man was he.
'Overhaul, overhaul, on your davit tackle fall,
And launch your boats to the sea'—brave boys,
    And launch your boats to the sea.

Now the boats were launched and the men a-board,
With the whalefish full in view;
Resolvéd were the whole boats' crews
To steer where the whalefish blew—brave boys,
    To steer where the whalefish blew.

And when we reached that whale, my boys,
He lashed out with his tail,
And we lost a boat, and seven good men,
And we never caught that whale—brave boys,
        And we never caught that whale.

Bad new, bad news, to our captain came,
That grieved him very sore.
But when he found that his cabin-boy was gone,
Why it grieved him ten times more—brave boys,
        It grieved him ten times more.

O, Greenland is an awful place,
Where the daylight's seldom seen,
Where there's ice, and there's snow, and the whalefishes
    blow,
Then *adieu* to cold Greenland—brave boys,
    Adieu to cold Greenland.

The Inchcape Rock

Robert Southey

No stir in the air, no stir in the sea,
The ship was as still as she could be,
Her sails from heaven received no motion,
Her keel was steady in the ocean.

Without either sign or sound of their shock
The waves flowed over the Inchcape Rock;
So little they rose, so little they fell,
They did not move the Inchcape Bell.

The Abbot of Aberbrothock
Had placed that bell on the Inchcape Rock;
On a buoy in the storm it floated and swung,
And over the waves its warning rung.

When the Rock was hid by the surge's swell
The mariners heard the warning bell;
And then they knew the perilous Rock
And blest the Abbot of Aberbrothock.

The sun in heaven was shining gay,
All things were joyful on that day;
The sea-birds screamed as they wheeled round,
And there was joyaunce in their sound.

The buoy of the Inchcape Bell was seen
A darker speck on the ocean green;
Sir Ralph the Rover walked his deck,
And he fixed his eye on the darker speck.

He felt the cheering power of spring,
It made him whistle, it made him sing,
His heart was mirthful to excess
But the Rover's mirth was wickedness.

His eye was on the Inchcape float;
Quoth he, 'My men, put out the boat,
And row me to the Inchcape Rock,
And I'll plague the Abbot of Aberbrothock.'

The boat is lowered, the boatmen row,
And to the Inchcape Rock they go;
Sir Ralph bent over from the boat,
And he cut the bell from the Inchcape float.

Down sank the bell with a gurgling sound,
The bubbles rose and burst around;
Quoth Sir Ralph, 'The next who comes to the Rock
Won't bless the Abbot of Aberbrothock.'

Sir Ralph the Rover sailed away,
He scoured the seas for many a day;
And now grown rich with plundered store,
He steers his course for Scotland's shore.

So thick a haze o'erspreads the sky
They cannot see the sun on high;
The wind hath blown a gale all day,
At evening it hath died away.

On the deck the Rover takes his stand,
So dark it is he sees no land.
Quoth Sir Ralph, 'It will be lighter soon,
For there is the dawn of the rising moon.'

'Canst hear,' said one, 'the breakers roar?
For methinks we should be near the shore.'
'Now where we are I cannot tell,
But I wish I could hear the Inchcape Bell.'

They hear no sound, the swell is strong;
Though the wind hath fallen they drift along;
Till the vessel strikes with a shivering shock—
'O Christ! it is the Inchcape Rock!'

Sir Ralph the Rover tore his hair;
He curst himself in his despair;
The waves rush in on every side,
The ship is sinking beneath the tide.

But even in his dying fear
One dreadful sound could the Rover hear,
A sound as if with the Inchcape Bell
The Devil below was ringing his knell.

Morgan

Edward Harrington

When Morgan crossed the Murray to Peechelba and
  doom
A sombre silent shadow rode with him through the
  gloom.
The wild things of the forest slunk from the outlaw's
  track,
The boobook croaked a warning, 'Go back, go back, go
  back!'
It woke no answering echo in Morgan's blackened soul,
As onward through the darkness he rode towards his
  goal.

An evil man was Morgan, a price was on his head;
The simple bush-folk whispered his very name with
  dread;
Before the fierce Dan Morgan the bravest man might
  quake—
A cold and callous killer, he killed for killing's sake.
Past swamp and creek and gully, and settler's lone
  abode,
Towards the station homestead the grim Dan Morgan
  rode.

And still that hooded horseman that Morgan could not
  see,
Watched by the wild bush-creatures, rode close beside
  his knee.
Before them in a clearing a drover's campfire burned:
The phantom rode with Morgan, and turned when
  Morgan turned.
And loud the boobook's warning came on the cold night
  air,
'Go back, go back, Dan Morgan. Beware, beware,
  beware!'

He reached the station homestead; into the hall he
	strode,
And on his evil features the flickering lamplight glowed.
'Into one room!' he thundered. 'Bring me a glass of
	grog!
If any disobey me I'll shoot him like a dog!'
With pistols cocked and ready, dark-eyed and
	beetle-browed—
Before the famous outlaw the bravest hearts were cowed.

All night with loaded pistols he dozed and muttered
	there,
All night the evil shadow stood close beside his chair.
The brave Scotch girl McDonald, a lass who knew no
	fear,
Slipped out unseen by Morgan to warn the homesteads
	near.
And in the hours of darkness, before the break of dawn,
Around the fierce Dan Morgan the fatal net was drawn.

Day broke upon the Murray, the morning mists were
	gone,
The magpies sang their matins, the river murmured on.
When Morgan left the homestead and neared the
	stockyard gate
He heard the boobook's warning, and turned but turned
	too late—
For Quinlan pressed the trigger as Morgan swung around,
And sent the grim bushranger blaspheming to the
	ground.

So fell the dread Dan Morgan in Eighteen sixty-five,
In death as much unpitied as hated when alive.
He lived by blood and plunder, an outlaw to the end;
In life he showed no mercy, in death he left no
	friend.
And all who seek to follow in Morgan's evil track
Should heed the boobook's warning: 'Go back, go back,
	go back!'

The Ballad of Billy Rose
Leslie Norris

Outside Bristol Rovers Football Ground—
The date has gone from me, but not the day,
Nor how the dissenting flags in stiff array
Stuck bravely out against the sky's grey round—

Near the Car Park then, past Austin and Ford,
Lagonda, Bentley, and a colourful patch
Of country coaches come in for the match
Was where I walked, having travelled the road

From Fishponds to watch Portsmouth in the Cup.
The Third Round, I believe. And I was filled
With the old excitement which had thrilled
Me so completely when, while growing up,

I went on Saturdays to match or fight.
Not only me; for thousands of us there
Strode forward eagerly, each man aware
Of vigorous memory, anticipating delight.

We all moved forward, all, except one man.
I saw him because he was paradoxically still,
A stone against the flood, face upright against us all,
Head bare, hoarse voice aloft. Blind as a stone.

I knew him at once despite his pathetic clothes—
Something in his stance, or his sturdy frame
Perhaps. I could even remember his name
Before I saw it on his blind-man's tray. Billy Rose.

And twenty forgetful years fell away at the sight.
Bare-kneed, dismayed, memory fled to the hub
Of Saturday violence, with friends to the Labour
       Club—
Watching the boxing on a sawdust summer night.

The boys' enclosure close to the shabby ring
Was where we stood, clenched in a resin world,
Spoke in cool voices, lounged, were artificially bored
During minor bouts. We paid threepence to go in.

Billy Rose fought there. He was top of the bill.
So brisk a fighter, so gallant, so precise!
Trim as a tree he stood for the ceremonies,
Then turned to meet George Morgan of Triphil.

He had no chance. Courage was not enough,
Nor tight defence. Donald Davies was sick
And we threatened his cowardice with an embarrassed
    kick.
Ripped across both his eyes was Rose, but we were
    tough

And clapped him as they wrapped his blindness up
In busy towels, applauded the wave
He gave his executioners, cheered the brave
Blind man as he cleared with a jaunty hop

The top rope. I had forgotten that day
As if it were dead for ever, yet now I saw
Again the flowers of blood on the ring floor
As bright as his name. I cannot say

How long I stood with ghosts of the wild fists
And the cries of shaken boys long dead around me,
For struck to act at last, in terror and pity
I threw some frantic money, three treacherous pence—

And I cry at the memory—into his tray, and ran,
Entering the waves of the stadium like a drowning man.
Poor Billy Rose. God, he could fight
Before my three sharp coins knocked out his sight.

Brennan on the Moor

Traditional

It's of a fearless highwayman a story I will tell;
His name was William Brennan and in Ireland he did
    dwell.
Upon the Libbery Mountains he commenced his wild
    career,
Where many a wealthy gentleman before him shook
    with fear.
> *Brennan on the moor! Brennan on the moor!*
> *Bold and undaunted stood Brennan on the moor!*

One day he robbed a packman and his name was Pedlar
    Bawn;
They travelled on together till the day began to dawn;
The pedlar found his money gone, likewise his watch
    and chain,
He at once encountered Brennan, and he robbed him
    back again.
> *Brennan on the moor! ...*

When Brennan saw the pedlar was as good a man
    as he,
He took him on the highway his companion to be;
The pedlar threw away his pack without any delay,
And proved a faithful comrade until his dying day.
> *Brennan on the moor! ...*

One day upon the King's highway as Willie he sat down,
He met the Mayor of Cashel just a mile outside the
    town;
The Mayor he knew his features: 'Oh, you're my man!'
    said he,
'I think you're William Brennan—you must come along
    with me!'
> *Brennan on the moor! ...*

Now Willie's wife had been to town provisions for to
     buy,
And when she saw her Willie she began to sob and cry;
He said, 'Give me that tenpence[1]!' and as quick as
     Willie spoke,
She handed him a blunderbuss from underneath her
     cloak.
          Brennan on the moor! ...

Now with this loaded blunderbuss, the truth I will
     unfold,
He made the Mayor to tremble, and he robbed him of
     his gold;
A hundred pounds was offered for his apprehension
     there,
But he with horse and saddle to the mountains did
     repair.
          Brennan on the moor! ...

He lay among the fern all day, 'twas thick upon the
     field,
And many wounds he did receive before that he would
     yield;
He was captured and found guilty, and the Judge made
     this reply:
'For robbing on the King's highway you are condemned
     to die!'
          Brennan on the moor! ...

1 Slang for a gun.

Return

Peter Roberts

The darkened Mess was silent. Nothing stirred.
The sounds which drifted in were muffled, blurred,
And often lost before they could be heard.
Two white-clad figures stood, without a word,
And listened to the whispering voice of night
Around the walls which hid the moon from sight.
The moonlight strayed across the hangar doors
And splashed in patches on the concrete floors;
A flarepath glimmered on the aerodrome;
The beacon flashed to guide the bombers home ...
And then the rustling night wind brought a sound
That muttered softly, swelled and then was drowned,
And for an endless moment silence reigned,
While in the silver darkness ears were strained
To catch that long expected sound anew ...
At last it came again, and quickly grew,
Its surging waves became a steady drone,
The world seemed filled with it, and it alone—
Gliding across the darkness overhead,
With lights at wing-tips gleaming, green and red,
The first dark shape of the returning band
With motors throttled back came in to land.

Now, warmly lit, the Mess was flooded through
With cheerful noise. Young men in dusty blue,
Bright scarves and heavy sweaters, eager-eyed,
Sat round the table. Everybody tried
To speak at once, and laughter strong and clear
Rang out across the room. Pint pots of beer
Were raised to thirsty lips, and once again
Nerves, braced against the threat of death and pain,
Relaxed, until the things that mattered most
Were eggs and bacon, jam and buttered toast,
And these the two white figures soon supplied.
But when at last, with hunger satisfied,

They rose and stretched themselves, and made for bed,
'Where's Jimmy? I've not seen him,' someone said.
And then the talking ceased, they looked around,
As if, by seeking, Jimmy could be found.
One saw the clock. 'Still half an hour to go.
He often cuts it pretty fine, you know.'
The lights were out, the tables in the room
Once more retreated deep into the gloom.
Again the very walls were listening,
And waiting for the stealthy wind to bring
Some murmur of the last returning crew.
The curtains fluttered gently, letting through
A sudden glimpse of swiftly setting moon.
And when the shadowed ridge of Sandham Hill
Turned purple in the dawning, all too soon,
The silent room was listening, listening still.

Matilda

who told lies, and was burned to death

Hilaire Belloc

Matilda told such Dreadful Lies,
It made one Gasp and Stretch one's Eyes;
Her Aunt, who from her Earliest Youth,
Had kept a Strict Regard for Truth,
Attempted to Believe Matilda:
The effort very nearly killed her,
And would have done so, had not She
Discovered this Infirmity.
For once, towards the Close of Day,
Matilda, growing tired of play,
And finding she was left alone,
Went tiptoe to the Telephone
And summoned the Immediate Aid
Of London's Noble Fire-Brigade.
Within an hour the Gallant Band
Were pouring in on every hand,
From Putney, Hackney Downs and Bow.
With Courage high and Hearts a-glow,
They galloped, roaring through the Town,
'Matilda's House is Burning Down!'
Inspired by British Cheers and Loud
Proceeding from the Frenzied Crowd,
They ran their ladders through a score
Of windows on the Ball Room Floor;
And took Peculiar Pains to Souse
The pictures up and down the House,
Until Matilda's Aunt succeeded
In showing them they were not needed;
And even then she had to pay
To get the Men to go away!
It happened that a few Weeks later
Her Aunt was off to the Theatre

To see that Interesting Play
The Second Mrs. Tanqueray.
She had refused to take her Niece
To hear that Entertaining Piece:
A Deprivation Just and Wise
To Punish her for Telling Lies.
That Night a Fire DID break out—
You should have heard Matilda Shout!
You should have heard her Scream and Bawl,
And throw the window up and call
To People passing in the Street—
(The rapidly increasing Heat
Encouraging her to obtain
Their confidence)—but all in vain!
For every time She shouted 'Fire!'
They only answered 'Little Liar!'
And therefore when her Aunt returned,
Matilda, and the House, were Burned.

⤷ WORD PICTURES ⤶

The Tiger

William Blake

Tiger! Tiger! burning bright
In the forests of the night,
What immortal hand or eye
Could frame thy fearful symmetry?

In what distant deeps or skies
Burnt the fire of thine eyes?
On what wings dare he aspire?
What the hand dare seize the fire?

And what shoulder, and what art,
Could twist the sinews of thy heart?
And when thy heart began to beat,
What dread hand? and what dread feet?

What the hammer? what the chain?
In what furnace was thy brain?
What the anvil? what dread grasp
Dare its deadly terrors clasp?

When the stars threw down their spears,
And watered heaven with their tears,
Did He smile His work to see?
Did He who made the Lamb make thee?

Tiger! Tiger! burning bright
In the forests of the night,
What immortal hand or eye
Dare frame thy fearful symmetry?

Circus

Margaret Stanley-Wrench

Saucer of sand, the circus ring,
A cup of light, clowns tumbling.

Horses with white manes sleek and streaming,
Bits jingling, tinkling, silk skins gleaming.

But there, shut in their iron cage,
Sulky, drowsy, dulled by rage

The lions beg or trot or leap,
And cringe like beaten dogs, and creep,

King beasts, who should be free to run
Through forests striped with shade and sun,

With fierce, proud eyes and manes like fire.
These manes hang dull like rusty wire.

And when the trainer cracks his whip
They snarl and curl a sullen lip,

And only in their dreams are free
To crush and kill man's cruelty.

The Red Cockatoo

Po Chu-I
(Translated from the Chinese by
Arthur Waley)

Sent as a present from Annam—
A red cockatoo.
Coloured like the peach-tree blossom,
Speaking with the speech of men.
And they did to it what is always done
To the learned and eloquent.
They took a cage with stout bars
And shut it up inside.

The Eagle

Alfred Lord Tennyson

He clasps the crag with crooked hands;
Close to the sun in lonely lands,
Ringed with the azure world he stands.

The wrinkled sea beneath him crawls;
He watches from his mountain walls,
And like a thunderbolt he falls.

Pigeons

Richard Kell

They paddle with staccato feet
in powder-pools of sunlight,
small blue busybodies
strutting like fat gentlemen
with hands clasped
under their swallowtail coats;
and as they stump about,
their heads like tiny hammers
tap at imaginary nails
in non-existent walls.

Elusive ghosts of sunshine
slither down the green gloss
of their necks an instant, and are gone.

Summer hangs drugged from sky to earth
in limpid fathoms of silence:
only warm dark dimples of sound
slide like slow bubbles
from the contented throats.

Raise a casual hand—
with one quick gust
they fountain into air.

The Robin

Thomas Hardy

When up aloft
I fly and fly,
I see in pools
The shining sky,
And a happy bird
Am I, am I!

When I descend
Towards their brink
I stand, and look,
And stoop, and drink,
And bathe my wings,
And chink and prink.

When winter frost
Makes earth as steel
I search and search
But find no meal,
And most unhappy
Then I feel.

But when it lasts,
And snows still fall,
I get to feel
No grief at all,
For I turn to a cold stiff
Feathery ball!

Feline

Melissa Gaye Wallen

A picture of grace,
As she springs on her prey—
In one swift movement
She whisks it away.
She tosses it up,
High into the air,
It turns once or twice
And is caught with great care.
Then she eats it.

She washes herself,
And then enters the house—
Having filled herself up
With a Morsel of Mouse.
Her master arrives—
She asks to be stroked,
Then his hand slips a bit
And she's highly provoked.
So she leaves him.

Her muscles are supple,
Her coat very glossy,
Her tail slim and tapered,
Her ears perked and saucy.
Her eyes are so azure,
They're blue as the sea—
Almond-shaped opals,
Pooled mystery.
A picture of grace.

The Woodman's Dog

William Cowper

Shaggy, and lean, and shrewd, with pointed ears,
And tail cropped short, half lurcher and half cur—
His dog attends him. Close behind his heel
Now creeps he slow; and now, with many a frisk
Wide-scampering, snatches up the drifted snow
With ivory teeth, or ploughs it with his snout;
Then shakes his powdered coat, and barks for joy.

Minnows

John Keats

Swarms of minnows show their little heads,
Staying their wavy bodies 'gainst the streams,
To taste the luxury of sunny beams
Tempered with coolness. How they ever wrestle
With their own sweet delight, and ever nestle
Their silver bellies on the pebbly sand.
If you but scantily hold out the hand,
That very instant not one will remain;
But turn your eye, and they are there again.

The Boy Fishing

E. J. Scovell

I am cold and alone,
On my tree-root sitting as still as a stone.
The fish come to my net. I scorned the sun,
The voices on the road, and they have gone.
My eyes are buried in the cold pond, under
The cold, spread leaves; my thoughts are silver-wet.
I have ten stickleback, a half-day's plunder,
Safe in my jar. I shall have ten more yet.

Timothy Winters

Charles Causley

Timothy Winters comes to school
With eyes as wide as a football-pool,
Ears like bombs and teeth like splinters:
A blitz of a boy is Timothy Winters.

His belly is white, his neck is dark,
And his hair is an exclamation mark.
His clothes are enough to scare a crow
And through his britches the blue winds blow.

When teacher talks he won't hear a word
And he shoots down dead the arithmetic-bird,
He licks the patterns off his plate
And he's not even heard of the Welfare State.

Timothy Winters has bloody feet
And he lives in a house on Suez Street,
He sleeps in a sack on the kitchen floor
And they say there aren't boys like him any more.

Old man Winters likes his beer
And his missus ran off with a bombardier,
Grandma sits in the grate with a gin
And Timothy's dosed with an aspirin.

The Welfare Worker lies awake
But the law's as tricky as a ten-foot snake,
So Timothy Winters drinks his cup
And slowly goes on growing up.

At Morning Prayers the Headmaster helves
For children less fortunate than ourselves,
And the loudest response in the room is when
Timothy Winters roars 'Amen!'

So come one angel, come on ten:
Timothy Winters says 'Amen'
Amen amen amen amen.
Timothy Winters, Lord.
        Amen.

Gipsies

John Clare

The gipsies seek wide sheltering woods again,
With droves of horses flock to mark their lane,
And trample on dead leaves, and hear the sound,
And look and see the black clouds gather round,
And set their camps, and free from muck and mire,
And gather stolen sticks to make the fire.
The roasted hedgehog, bitter though as gall,
Is eaten up and relished by them all.
They know the woods and every fox's den
And get their living far away from men;
The shooters ask them where to find the game,
The rabbits know them and are almost tame.
The aged women, tawny with the smoke,
Go with the winds and crack the rotted oak.

The Farmer

Flexmore Hudson

Star-mist was on the hills; the cows had been fed.
It was twilight, soft and windless,
and the trees in the west tipped with red.
I walked with the farmer through the fallows,
while the dogs drove the sheep ahead.
We had to shout in that babble of lambs bleating
in long bursts of hunger that fell into hushes,
while the ewes ran from lamb to lamb frenziedly
        sniffing,
searching with strange little rushes,
and the rams turned to stamp at the dogs.
And though I had lived with the man in his home,
seen him a thousand times with his children and wife,
I had not known before such tenderness to come
into his face as he raised a sick lamb from its rest
and, folding its forelegs gently, carried it close to his
        breast.

Old Johnny Armstrong

Raymond Wilson

Old Johnny Armstrong's eighty or more
And he humps like a question-mark
Over two gnarled sticks as he shuffles and picks
His slow way to Benwell Park.

He's lived in Benwell his whole life long
And remembers how street-lights came,
And how once on a time they laid a tram-line,
Then years later dug up the same!

Now he's got to take a lift to his flat,
Up where the tall winds blow
Round a Council Block that rears like a rock
From seas of swirled traffic below.

Old Johnny Armstrong lives out his life
In his cell on the seventeenth floor,
And it's seldom a neighbour will do him a favour
Or anyone knock at his door.

With his poor hands knotted with rheumatism
And his poor back doubled in pain,
Why, day after day, should he pick his slow way
To Benwell Park yet again?—

O the wind in park trees is the self-same wind
That first blew on a village child
When life freshly unfurled in a green, lost world
And his straight limbs ran wild.

Composed upon Westminster Bridge September 3rd, 1802

William Wordsworth

Earth has not anything to show more fair:
Dull would he be of soul who could pass by
A sight so touching in its majesty:
This City now doth like a garment wear
The beauty of the morning: silent, bare,
Ships, towers, domes, theatres, and temples lie
Open unto the fields, and to the sky;
All bright and glittering in the smokeless air.

Never did sun more beautifully steep
In his first splendour valley, rock, or hill;
Ne'er saw I, never felt, a calm so deep.
The river glideth at his own sweet will:
Dear God! the very houses seem asleep;
And all that mighty heart is lying still.

Clearing at Dawn

Li Po
(Translated from the Chinese by Arthur
Waley)

The fields are chill, the sparse rain has stopped;
The colours of spring teem on every side.
With leaping fish the blue pond is full;
With singing thrushes the green boughs droop.
The flowers of the field have dabbled their powdered
       cheeks;
The mountain grasses are bent level at the waist.
By the bamboo stream the last fragment of cloud
Blown by the wind slowly scatters away.

Weathers

Thomas Hardy

This is the weather the cuckoo likes,
     And so do I;
When showers betumble the chestnut spikes,
     And nestlings fly:
And the little brown nightingale bills his best,
And they sit outside at 'The Travellers' Rest',
And maids come forth sprig-muslin drest,
And citizens dream of the south and west,
     And so do I.

This is the weather the shepherd shuns,
     And so do I;
When beeches drip in browns and duns,
     And thresh, and ply;
And hill-hid tides throb, throe on throe,
And meadow rivulets overflow,
And drops on gate-bars hang in a row,
And rooks in families homeward go,
     And so do I.

Water Picture

May Swenson

In the pond in the park
all things are doubled:
long buildings hang and
wriggle gently. Chimneys
are bent legs bouncing
on clouds below. A flag
wags like a fishhook
down there in the sky.

The arched stone bridge
is an eye, with underlid
in the water. In its lens
dip crinkled heads with hats
that don't fall off. Dogs go by,
barking on their backs.
A baby, taken to feed the
ducks, dangles upside-down,
a pink balloon for a buoy.

Treetops deploy a haze of
cherry bloom for roots,
where birds coast belly-up
in the glass bowl of a hill;
from its bottom a bunch
of peanut-munching children
is suspended by their
sneakers, waveringly.

A swan, with twin necks
forming the figure three,
steers between two dimpled
towers doubled. Fondly,
hissing, she kisses herself,
and all the scene is troubled:
water-windows splinter,
tree-limbs tangle, the bridge
folds like a fan.

A Hot Day

A. S. J. Tessimond

Cottonwool clouds loiter.
A lawnmower, very far,
Birrs. Then a bee comes
To a crimson rose and softly,
Deftly and fatly crams
A velvet body in.

A tree, June-lazy, makes
A tent of dim green light.
Sunlight weaves in the leaves,
Honey-light laced with leaf-light,
Green interleaved with gold.
Sunlight gathers its rays
In sheaves, which the wind unweaves
And then reweaves—the wind
That puffs a smell of grass
Through the heat-heavy, trembling
Summer pool of air.

Thunder and Lightning

James Kirkup

Blood punches through every vein
As lightning strips the windowpane.

Under its flashing whip, a white
Village leaps to light.

On tubs of thunder, fists of rain
Slog it out of sight again.

Blood punches the heart with fright
As rain belts the village night.

Autumn

John Clare

I love the fitful gust that shakes
        The casement all the day,
And from the glossy elm tree takes
        The faded leaves away,
Twirling them by the window pane
With thousand others down the lane.

I love to see the shaking twig
        Dance till shut of eve,
The sparrow on the cottage rig,
        Whose chirp would make believe
That spring was just now flirting by
In Summer's lap with flowers to lie.

I love to see the cottage smoke
        Curl upwards through the trees;
The pigeons nestled round the cote
        On November days like these;
The cock upon the dunghill crowing,
The mill sails on the heath a-going.

Symphony in Yellow

Oscar Wilde

An omnibus across the bridge
Crawls like a yellow butterfly,
And, here and there, a passer-by
Shows like a little restless midge.

Big barges full of yellow hay
Are moved against the shadowy wharf,
And, like a yellow silken scarf,
The thick fog hangs along the quay.

The yellow leaves begin to fade
And flutter from the Temple elms,
And at my feet the pale green Thames
Lies like a rod of rippled jade.

New York Skyscrapers

John Mbiti

The weak scattered rays of yellow sun
Peeped through the hazy tissues
That blanketed them with transparent wax;
And as the wrinkled rays closed the day,
Smoky chimneys of New York coughed
Looking down in bended towers
And vomited sad tears of dark smoke.

November

John Clare

The shepherds almost wonder where they dwell,
And the old dog for his right journey stares:
The path leads somewhere, but they cannot tell,
And neighbour meets with neighbour unawares.
The maiden passes close beside her cow,
And wanders on, and thinks her far away;
The ploughman goes unseen behind his plough
And seems to lose his horses half the day.
The lazy mist creeps on in journey slow;
The maidens shout and wonder where they go;
So dull and dark are the November days.
The lazy mist high up the evening curled,
And now the morn quite hides in smoke and haze;
The place we occupy seems all the world.

57

November Night

Adelaide Crapsey

Listen. . . .
With faint dry sound,
Like steps of passing ghosts,
The leaves, frost-crisped, break from the trees
And fall.

Fireworks

James Reeves

They rise like sudden fiery flowers
      That burst upon the night,
Then fall to earth in burning showers
      Of crimson, blue, and white.

Like buds too wonderful to name,
      Each miracle unfolds,
And catherine-wheels begin to flame
      Like whirling marigolds.

Rockets and Roman candles make
      An orchard of the sky,
Whence magic trees their petals shake
      Upon each gazing eye.

The Snowflake

Walter de la Mare

Before I melt
Come, look at me!
This lovely icy filigree!
Of a great forest
In one night
I make a wilderness
Of white:
By skyey cold
Of crystals made,
All softly, on
Your finger laid,
I pause, that you
My beauty see:
Breathe, and I vanish
Instantly.

Snow

Edward Thomas

In the gloom of whiteness,
In the great silence of snow,
A child was sighing
And bitterly saying: 'Oh,
They have killed a white bird up there on her nest,
The down is fluttering from her breast!'
And still it fell through that dusky brightness
On the child crying for the bird of the snow.

Last Snow

Andrew Young

Although the snow still lingers
Heaped on the ivy's blunt webbed fingers
And painted tree-trunks on one side,
Here in this sunlit ride
The fresh unchristened things appear,
Leaf, spathe and stem,
With crumbs of earth clinging to them
To show the way they came
But no flower yet to tell their name,
And one green spear
Stabbing a dead leaf from below
Kills winter at a blow.

The Fog

F. R. McCreary

Slowly the fog,
Hunch-shouldered, with a grey face,
Arms wide, advances,
Finger-tips touching the way
Past the dark houses
And dark gardens of roses
Up the short street from the harbour,
Slowly the fog,
Seeking, seeking;
Arms wide, shoulders hunched,
Searching, searching.
Out through the streets to the fields,
Slowly the fog—
A blind man hunting the moon.

Midnight Wood

Raymond Wilson

Dark in the wood the shadows stir:
  What do you see? —
Mist and moonlight, star and cloud,
Hunchback shapes that creep and crowd
  From tree to tree.

Dark in the wood a thin wind calls:
  What do you hear? —
Frond and fern and clutching grass
Snigger at you as you pass,
  Whispering fear.

Dark in the wood a river flows:
  What does it hide? —
Otter, water-rat, old tin can,
Bones of fish and bones of a man
  Drift in its tide.

Dark in the wood the owlets shriek:
  What do they cry? —
Choose between the wood and river;
Who comes here is lost for ever,
  And must die!

The Dismantled Ship
Walt Whitman

In some unused lagoon, some nameless bay,
On sluggish, lonesome waters, anchored near the shore,
An old, dismasted, grey and battered ship, disabled,
      done,
After free voyages to all the seas of earth, hauled up at
      last and hawsered tight,
Lies rusting, mouldering.

HMS Hero
Michael Roberts

Pale grey, her guns hooded, decks clear of all
      impediment,
Easily, between the swart tugs, she glides in the pale
      October sunshine:
It is Saturday afternoon, and the men are at football,
The wharves and the cobbled streets are silent by the
      slow river.

Smoothly, rounding the long bend, she glides to her
      place in history,
Past the grimed windows cracked and broken,
Past Swan Hunter's, Hawthorn Leslie's, Armstrong's,
Down to the North Sea, and trials, and her first
      commission.
Here is grace; and a job well done; built only for one
      end.
Women watch from the narrow doorways and give no
      sign,
Children stop playing by the wall and stare in silence
At gulls wheeling above the Tyne, or the ship passing.

from The Great Lover

Rupert Brooke

These I have loved:
                  White plates and cups, clean-gleaming,
Ringed with blue lines; and feathery, faery dust;
Wet roofs, beneath the lamp-light; the strong crust
Of friendly bread; and many-tasting food;
Rainbows; and the blue bitter smoke of wood;
And radiant raindrops couching in cool flowers;
And flowers themselves, that sway through sunny hours,
Dreaming of moths that drink them under the moon;
Then, the cool kindliness of sheets, that soon
Smooth away trouble; and the rough male kiss
Of blankets; grainy wood; live hair that is
Shining and free; blue-massing clouds; the keen
Unpassioned beauty of a great machine;
The benison of hot water; furs to touch;
The good smell of old clothes; and other such—
The comfortable smell of friendly fingers,
Hair's fragrance, and the musty reek that lingers
About dead leaves and last year's ferns. . . .

                           Dear names,
And thousand other throng to me! Royal flames;
Sweet water's dimpling laugh from tap or spring;
Holes in the ground; and voices that do sing;
Voices in laughter, too; and body's pain,
Soon turned to peace; and the deep-panting train;
Firm sands; the little dulling edge of foam
That browns and dwindles as the wave goes home;
And washen stones, gay for an hour; the cold
Graveness of iron; moist black earthen mould;
Sleep; and high places; footprints in the dew;
And oaks; and brown horse-chestnuts, glossy-new;
And new-peeled sticks; and shining pools on grass;—
All these have been my loves.

Spray

D. H. Lawrence

It is a wonder foam is so beautiful.
A wave bursts in anger on a rock, broken up
in wild white sibilant spray
and falls back, drawing in its breath with rage,
with frustration how beautiful!

Miracles

Walt Whitman

Why, who makes much of a miracle?
As to me I know of nothing else but miracles,
Whether I walk the streets of Manhattan,
Or dart my sight over the roofs of houses toward the
      sky,
Or wade with naked feet along the beach just in the
      edge of the water,
Or stand under trees in the woods,
Or talk by day with anyone I love,
Or sit at table at dinner with the rest,
Or look at strangers opposite me riding in the car,
Or watch honey-bees busy around the hive of summer
      forenoon,
Or animals feeding in the fields,
Or birds, or the wonderfulness of insects in the air,
Or the wonderfulness of the sundown,
Or of stars shining so quiet and bright,
Or the exquisite, delicate, thin curve of the new moon
      in spring;
These with the rest, one and all, are to me miracles. . .

♪ SONG AND DANCE ♪

Introduction to
Songs of Innocence
William Blake

Piping down the valleys wild,
Piping songs of pleasant glee,
On a cloud I saw a child,
And he laughing said to me:

'Pipe a song about a Lamb!'
So I piped with merry cheer.
'Piper, pipe that song again;'
So I piped: he wept to hear.

'Drop thy pipe, thy happy pipe;
Sing thy songs of happy cheer:'
So I sang the same again,
While he wept with joy to hear.

'Piper, sit thee down and write
In a book, that all may read.'
So he vanished from my sight,
And I plucked a hollow reed,

And I made a rural pen,
And I stained the water clear,
And I wrote my happy songs
Every child may joy to hear.

The Rivals

James Stephens

I heard a bird at dawn
Singing sweetly on a tree,
That the dew was on the lawn,
And the wind was on the lea!
But I didn't listen to him,
For he didn't sing to me!

I didn't listen to him,
For he didn't sing to me
That the dew was on the lawn,
And the wind was on the lea!
I was singing all the time
Just as prettily as he!

I was singing all the time,
Just as prettily as he,
About the dew upon the lawn,
And the wind upon the lea!
So I didn't listen to him
As he sang upon a tree!

Lord of the Dance

Sidney Carter

I danced in the morning
When the world was begun,
And I danced in the moon
And the stars and the sun,
And I came down from heaven
And I danced on the earth—
At Bethlehem I had my birth.

68

Dance then wherever you may be,
I am the Lord of the Dance, said he,
And I'll lead you all, wherever you may be
And I'll lead you all in the dance, said he.

I danced for the scribe
And the pharisee,
But they would not dance
And they wouldn't follow me,
I danced for the fishermen,
For James and John—
They came with me
And the dance went on.

I danced on the Sabbath,
And I cured the lame,
The holy people
Said it was a shame;
They whipped and they stripped
And they hung me high,
And they left me there
On a Cross to die.

I danced on a Friday
When the sky turned black—
It's hard to dance
With the devil on your back;
They buried my body
And they thought I'd gone—
But I am the dance
And I still go on.

They cut me down
And I leap up high—
I am the life
That'll never, never die;
I'll live in you
If you'll live in me,
I am the Lord
Of the Dance, said he.

The Dancing Cabman

J. B. Morton

Alone on the lawn
The cabman dances;
In the dew of dawn
He kicks and prances.

His bowler is set
On his bullet head,
For his boots are wet,
And his aunt is dead.

There on the lawn
As the light advances,
On the tide of the dawn,
The cabman dances.

Swift and strong
As a garden roller,
He dances along
In his little bowler.

Skimming the lawn
With royal grace,
The dew of the dawn
On his great red face.

To fairy flutes,
As the light advances,
In square black boots
The cabman dances.

Everyone Sang

Siegfried Sassoon

Everyone suddenly burst out singing;
And I was filled with such delight
As prisoned birds must find in freedom
Winging wildly across the white
Orchards and dark green fields; on—on—and out of
      sight.

Everyone's voice was suddenly lifted,
And beauty came like the setting sun.
My heart was shaken with tears, and horror
Drifted away . . . O, but Everyone
Was a bird; and the song was wordless; the singing will
      never be done.

The Fiddler of Dooney

W. B. Yeats

When I play on my fiddle in Dooney,
Folk dance like a wave of the sea;
My cousin is priest in Kilvarnet,
My brother in Mocharabuiee,

I passed my brother and cousin:
They read in their books of prayer;
I read in my book of songs
I bought at the Sligo fair.

When we come at the end of time
To Peter sitting in state,
He will smile on the three old spirits,
But call me first through the gate;

For the good are always the merry,
Save by an evil chance,
And the merry love the fiddle,
And the merry love to dance.

And when the folk there spy me,
They will all come up to me,
With, 'Here is the Fiddler of Dooney!'
And dance like a wave of the sea.

Polly Perkins

Unknown

I am a broken-hearted milkman, in grief I'm arrayed,
Through keeping of the company of a young servant
     maid,
Who lived on board and wages the house to keep clean
In a gentleman's family near Paddington Green.

Chorus
>*She was as beautiful as a butterfly*
>*And as proud as a Queen*
>*Was pretty little Polly Perkins*
>*Of Paddington Green.*

She'd an ankle like an antelope and a step like a deer,
A voice like a blackbird, so mellow and clear,
Her hair hung in ringlets so beautiful and long,
I thought that she loved me but I found I was wrong.

When I'd rattle in a morning and cry 'milk below',
At the sound of my milk-cans her face she would show
With a smile upon her countenance and a laugh in her
     eye,
If I thought she'd have loved me, I'd have laid down to
     die.

When I asked her to marry me she said 'Oh! what stuff!'
And told me to 'drop it, for she had quite enough
Of my nonsense'—at the same time I'd been very kind,
But to marry a milkman she didn't feel inclined.

'Oh, the man that has me must have silver and gold,
A chariot to ride in and be handsome and bold,
His hair must be curly as any watch spring,
And his whiskers as big as a brush for clothing.'

74

The words that she uttered went straight through my
      heart,
I sobbed, I sighed, and straight did depart;
With a tear on my eyelid as big as a bean,
Bidding good-bye to Polly and Paddington Green.

In six months she married, this hard-hearted girl,
But it was not a Wi-count, and it was not a Nearl,
It was not a 'Baronite', but a shade or two wuss,
It was a bow-legged conductor of a twopenny bus.

A Piper

Seumas O'Sullivan

A piper in the streets today
Set up and tuned, and started to play,
And away, away, away on the tide
Of his music we started; on every side
Doors and windows were opened wide,
And men left down their work and came,
And women with petticoats coloured like flame
And little bare feet that were blue with cold,
Went dancing back to the age of gold,
And all the world went gay, went gay,
For half an hour in the street today.

Tarantella

Hilaire Belloc

Do you remember an Inn,
Miranda?
Do you remember an Inn?
And the tedding and the spreading
Of the straw for a bedding,
And the fleas that tease in the High Pyrenees,
And the wine that tasted of the tar?
And the cheers and the jeers of the young muleteers
(Under the vine of the dark verandah)?
Do you remember an Inn, Miranda,
Do you remember an Inn?
And the cheers and the jeers of the young muleteers
Who hadn't got a penny,
And who weren't paying any,
And the hammer at the doors and the din?
And the Hip! Hop! Hap!
Of the clap
Of the hands to the twirl and the swirl
Of the girl gone chancing,
Glancing,
Dancing,
Backing and advancing,
Snapping of the clapper to the spin
Out and in—
And the Ting, Tong, Tang of the guitar!
Do you remember an Inn,
Miranda?
Do you remember an Inn?

Never more;
Miranda,
Never more.
Only the high peaks hoar:
And Aragon a torrent at the door.
No sound

In the walls of the halls where falls
The tread
Of the feet of the dead to the ground.
No sound:
Only the boom
Of the far waterfall like doom.

Lachlan Gorach's Rhyme

Unknown

First the heel,
And then the toe,
That's the way
The polka goes.

First the toe,
And then the heel,
That's the way
To dance a reel.

Quick about,
And then away,
Lightly dance
The glad Strathspey.

Jump a jump,
And jump it big,
That's the way
To dance a jig.

Slowly, smiling,
As in France,
Follow through
The country dance.

Leave Her, Johnny

A Sea Shanty

I thought I heard the captain say:
>> Leave her, Johnny, leave her;
You may go ashore and touch your pay,
>> It's time for us to leave her.

The winds were foul, the trip was long;
>> Leave her, Johnny, leave her;
But before we go we'll sing a song,
>> It's time for us to leave her.

The winds were foul, the work was hard—
>> Leave her, Johnny, leave her—
From Liverpool Docks to Brooklyn Yard;
>> It's time for us to leave her.

She'd neither steer, nor stay, nor wear:
>> Leave her, Johnny, leave her;
She shipped it green and made us swear:
>> It's time for us to leave her.

She'd neither wear, nor steer, nor stay:
>> Leave her, Johnny, leave her;
Her running rigging carried away:
>> It's time for us to leave her.

The Song of the Whale

Kit Wright

Heaving mountain in the sea,
Whale, I heard you
Grieving.

Great whale, crying for your life,
Crying for your kind, I knew
How we would use
Your dying:

Lipstick for our painted faces,
Polish for our shoes.

Tumbling mountain in the sea,
Whale, I heard you
Calling.

Bird-high notes, keening, soaring:
At their edge a tiny drum
Like a heartbeat.

We would make you
Dumb.

In the forest of the sea,
Whale, I heard you
Singing,

Singing to your kind.
We'll never let you be.
Instead of life we choose

Lipstick for our painted faces
Polish for our shoes.

A Smuggler's Song

Rudyard Kipling

If you wake at midnight, and hear a horse's feet,
Don't go drawing back the blind, or looking in the
      street,
Them that asks no questions isn't told a lie.
Watch the wall, my darling, while the Gentlemen go by!
        Five and twenty ponies
        Trotting through the dark—
        Brandy for the Parson,
        'Baccy for the Clerk;
        Laces for a lady, letters for a spy,
And watch the wall, my darling, while the Gentlemen
      go by!

Running round the woodlump if you chance to find
Little barrels, roped and tarred, all full of brandy-wine;
Don't you shout to come and look, nor use 'em for your
      play.
Put the brushwood back again—and they'll be gone next
      day!

If you see the stable-door setting open wide;
If you see a tired horse lying down inside;
If your mother mends a coat cut about and tore;
If the lining's wet and warm—don't you ask no more!

If you meet King George's men, dressed in blue and
      red,
You be careful what you say, and mindful what is said.
If they call you 'pretty maid', and chuck you 'neath the
      chin,
Don't you tell where no one is, nor yet where no one's
      been!

Knocks and footsteps round the house—whistles after
      dark—
You've no call for running out till the house-dogs bark.

Trusty's here, and *Pincher's* here, and see how dumb
      they lie—
They don't fret to follow when the Gentlemen go by!

If you do as you've been told, likely there's a chance
You'll be give a dainty doll, all the way from France,
With a cap of Valenciennes, and a velvet hood—
A present from the Gentlemen, along o' being good!
          Five and twenty ponies
          Trotting through the dark—
          Brandy for the Parson,
          'Baccy for the Clerk.
Them that asks no questions isn't told a lie—
Watch the wall, my darling, while the Gentlemen go by!

Blue Jeans and Silver Guitars

Gerard Benson

The singer sang honeyed words,
    'Your eyes are dreaming!'
And heard the pressed-together girls
    Sighing and screaming.

When he thrashed the tightened strings
    Of his silver guitar
The excited electric sounds
    Throbbed to a star.

The star with the speed of a dream
    Flew to the eyes
Of a listening girl, who became
    Suddenly wise.

With the knowledge of a million years
    She danced in each limb;
The singer saw her star-lit eyes
    Looking at him;

Two eyes that were fed with his words
    In all that crowd
Of pretty, blue-jeaned, swaying girls
    Sang out aloud!

The singer sang truthful words,
    'There are stars in your eyes!'
And heard the pressed-together girls,
    Their screams, their sighs.

Daniel

Vachel Lindsay

Darius the Mede was a king and a wonder.
His eye was proud, and his voice was thunder.
He kept bad lions in a monstrous den.
He fed up the lions on Christian men.

Daniel was the chief hired man of the land.
He stirred up the jazz in the palace band.
He whitewashed the cellar. He shovelled in the coal.
And Daniel kept a-praying: 'Lord, save my soul.'
Daniel kept a-praying: 'Lord, save my soul.'
Daniel kept a-praying: 'Lord, save my soul.'

Daniel was the butler, swagger and swell.
He ran upstairs. He answered the bell.
And *he* would let in whoever came a-calling,
Saints so holy, scamps so appalling.
'Old man Ahab leaves his card.
Elisha and the bears are a-waiting in the yard.
Here comes Pharaoh and his snakes a-calling.
Here comes Cain and his wife a-calling.
Shadrach, Meshach and Abednego for tea.
Here comes Jonah and the whale,
And the *Sea!*
Here comes St Peter and his fishing-pole.
Here comes Judas and his silver a-calling,
Here comes old Beelzebub a-calling.'
And Daniel kept a-praying: 'Lord, save my soul.'
Daniel kept a-praying: 'Lord, save my soul.'
Daniel kept a-praying: 'Lord, save my soul.'

His sweetheart and his mother were Christian and
     meek.
They washed and ironed for Darius every week.
One Thursday he met them at the door:
Paid them as usual, but acted sore.

He said: 'Your Daniel is a dead little pigeon.
He's a good hard worker, but he talks religion.'
And he showed them Daniel in the lion's cage.
Daniel standing quietly, the lions in a rage.

His good old mother cried:
'Lord, save him.'
And Daniel's tender sweetheart cried:
'Lord, save him.'
And she was a golden lily in the dew.
And she was as sweet as an apple on the tree.
And she was as fine as a melon in the corn-field,
Gliding and lovely as a ship on the sea,
Gliding and lovely as a ship on the sea.
And she prayed to the Lord:
'*Send* Gabriel. *Send* Gabriel.'

King Darius said to the lions:
'Bite Daniel. Bite Daniel.
Bite him. Bite him. Bite him.'

Thus roared the lions:
'We want Daniel, Daniel, Daniel,
We want Daniel, Daniel, Daniel.
Grrrrrrrrrrrrrrrrrr
Grrrrrrrrrrrrrrrrrrr.'

And Daniel did not frown,
Daniel did not cry.
He kept on looking at the sky.

And the Lord said to Gabriel:
'Go chain the lions down,
Go chain the lions down,
Go chain the lions down,
Go chain the lions down.'
And *Gabriel* chained the lions,
And *Gabriel* chained the lions,
And *Gabriel* chained the lions,
And Daniel got out of the den,

And Daniel got out of the den,
And Daniel got out of the den.
And Darius said: 'You're a Christian child',
Darius said: 'You're a Christian child',
Darius said: 'You're a Christian child',
And gave him his job again,
And gave him his job again,
And gave him his job again.

Notting Hill Polka
W. Bridges-Adam

We've—had—
A Body in the house
    Since father passed away:
He took bad on
Saturday night an' he
    Went the followin' day.

Mum's—pulled—
The blinds all down
    An' bought some Sherry Wine,
An' we've put the tin
What the Arsenic's in
    At the bottom of the Ser-pen-tine!

Jean Richepin's Song

Herbert Trench

A poor lad once and a lad so trim,
  Fol de rol de raly O!
  Fol de rol!
A poor lad once and a lad so trim
Gave his love to her that loved not him.

And, says she, 'Fetch me to-night, you rogue,'
  Fol de rol de raly O!
  Fol de rol!
And, says she, 'Fetch me to-night, you rogue,
Your mother's heart to feed my dog!'

To his mother's house went that young man,
  Fol de rol de raly O!
  Fol de rol!
To his mother's house went that young man,
Killed her, and took the heart, and ran.

And as he was running, look you, he fell,
  Fol de rol de raly O!
  Fol de rol!
And as he was running, look you, he fell,
And the heart rolled on the ground as well.

And the lad, as the heart was a-rolling, heard
  Fol de rol de raly O!
  Fol de rol!
And the lad, as the heart was a-rolling, heard
That the heart was speaking, and this was the word;

The heart was a-weeping, and crying so small
  Fol de rol de raly O!
  Fol de rol!
The heart was a-weeping, and crying so small,
'Are you hurt, my child, are you hurt at all?'

Robin's Song

Rodney Bennett

Robins sang in England,
    Frost or rain or snow,
All the long December days
    Endless years ago.

Robins sang in England
    Before the Legions came,
Before our English fields were tilled
    Or England was a name.

Robins sang in England
    When forests dark and wild
Stretched across from sea to sea
    And Jesus was a child.

Listen! in the frosty dawn
    From his leafless bough
The same brave song he ever sang
    A robin's singing now.

I Sing of a Maiden

Unknown

I sing of a maiden
That is makeless[1],
King of all kings
To her son she ches[2].

He came all so still
Where his mother was,
As dew in April
That falleth on the grass.

He came all so still
Where his mother lay,
As dew in April
That falleth on the spray.

He came all so still
To his mother's bower,
As dew in April
That falleth on the flower.

Mother and maiden
Was never none but she;
Well may such a maiden
God's mother be.

1 Matchless, unequalled. 2 Chose.

O Child beside the Waterfall

George Barker

O Child beside the Waterfall
what songs without a word
rise from those waters like the call
only a heart has heard—
the Joy, the Joy in all things
rise whistling like a bird.

O Child beside the Waterfall
I hear them too, the brief
heavenly notes, the harp of dawn,
the nightingale on the leaf,
all, all dispel the darkness and
the silence of our grief.

O Child beside the Waterfall
I see you standing there
with waterdrops and fireflies
and hummingbirds in the air,
all singing praise of paradise,
paradise everywhere.

On Her Dancing

James Shirley

I stood and saw my mistress dance,
       Silent, and with so fixed an eye,
Some might suppose me in a trance.
       But being askéd why,
By one that knew I was in love,
       I could not but impart
My wonder, to behold her move
So nimbly with a marble heart.

Gypsy Dance

Linda Davies (aged 11)

I saw the gypsy queen
Dancing the flamenco,
Her flowing skirts changing, luminous in the light of the
      fire,
That rough black flowing mane twisting.
She jumped,
Oh how she jumped over that bitter roaring fire.
All the gypsy folk,
Their faces black in the shadows,
Waited.
Then, she fell on her knees
As though she were praying to God in the highest.
Oh how the gypsy folk clapped.
They clapped as hard as the moon shone.

Witches' Chant

William Shakespeare

First Witch

> Round about the cauldron go:
> In the poisoned entrails throw.
> Toad, that under cold stone
> Days and nights has thirty-one
> Sweated venom sleeping got,
> Boil thou first in the charmèd pot.

All

> Double, double, toil and trouble;
> Fire burn and cauldron bubble.

Second Witch

> Eye of newt and toe of frog,
> Wool of bat and tongue of dog,
> Adder's fork and blindworm's sting,
> Lizard's leg and owlet's wing.

All

> Double, double, toil and trouble;
> Fire burn and cauldron bubble.

Third Witch

> Scale of dragon, tooth of wolf,
> Witch's mummy, maw and gulf
> Of the ravenous salt-sea shark,
> Root of hemlock digged in the dark,
> Make the gruel thick and slab:
> Add thereto a tiger's chaudron,
> For the ingredients of our cauldron.

All

> Double, double, toil and trouble,
> Fire burn and cauldron bubble.

The Singing Cat

Stevie Smith

It was a little captive cat
      Upon a crowded train
His mistress takes him from his box
      To ease his fret and pain.

She holds him tight upon her knee
      The graceful animal
And all the people look at him
      He is so beautiful.

But oh he pricks and oh he prods
      And turns upon her knee
Then lifteth up his innocent voice
      In plaintive melody.

He lifteth up his innocent voice
      He lifteth up, he singeth
And to each human countenance
      A smile of grace he bringeth.

He lifteth up his innocent paw
      Upon her breast he clingeth
And everybody cries, Behold
      The cat, the cat that singeth.

He lifteth up his innocent voice
      He lifteth up, he singeth
And all the people warm themselves
      In the love his beauty bringeth.

Blow, Bugle, Blow

Song from 'The Princess'

Alfred Lord Tennyson

The splendour falls on castle walls
And snowy summits old in story:
The long light shakes across the lakes
And the wild cataract leaps in glory.
Blow, bugle, blow, set the wild echoes flying,
Blow, bugle; answer, echoes, dying, dying, dying.

O hark, O hear! how thin and clear,
And thinner, clearer, farther going!
O sweet and far from cliff and scar
The horns of Elfland faintly blowing!
Blow, let us hear the purple glens replying:
Blow, bugle; answer, echoes, dying, dying, dying.

O love, they die in yon rich sky,
They faint on hill or field or river;
Our echoes roll from soul to soul,
And grow for ever and for ever.
Blow, bugle, blow, set the wild echoes flying,
And answer, echoes, answer, dying, dying, dying.

Waltzing Matilda[1]

Andrew Barton Paterson

Once a jolly swagman[2] camped by a billabong[3]
    Under the shade of a coolibah[4] tree,
And he sang as he watched and waited till his billy[5]
    boiled,
    'You'll come a-waltzing Matilda with me!'
Waltzing Matilda, waltzing Matilda,
    You'll come a-waltzing Matilda with me:
And he sang as he watched and waited till his billy
    boiled,
    'You'll come a-waltzing Matilda with me!'

Down came a jumbuck[6] to drink at the billabong,
    Up jumped the swagman and grabbed him with
    glee,
And he sang as he stowed that jumbuck in his tucker[7]
    bag,
    'You'll come a-waltzing Matilda with me!'
Waltzing Matilda, waltzing Matilda
    You'll come a-waltzing Matilda with me:
And he sang as he stowed that jumbuck in his tucker
    bag,
    'You'll come a-waltzing Matilda with me!'

Up rode the squatter[8] mounted on his thoroughbred,
    Up rode the troopers, one, two, three.
'Where's that jolly jumbuck you've got in your tucker
    bag?
    You'll come a-waltzing Matilda with me!'

---

1 To tramp about the countryside carrying swag (stolen goods).
2 A casual worker. 3 A stagnant pool. 4 An Australian eucalyptus.
5 A kettle used in camp cooking. 6 A sheep. 7 Food. 8 A sheep-farmer.

Waltzing Matilda, waltzing Matilda,
    You'll come a-waltzing Matilda with me:
'Where's that jolly jumbuck you've got in your tucker
        bag?
    You'll come a-waltzing Matilda with me!'

Up jumped the swagman and sprang into the billabong,
    'You'll never take me alive!' said he.
And his ghost may be heard as you pass by that
        billabong,
    'You'll never take me alive!' said he.
Waltzing Matilda, waltzing Matilda,
    You'll come a-waltzing Matilda with me,
And his ghost may be heard as you pass by that
        billabong,
    'You'll come a-waltzing Matilda with me!'

To Dance upon the Air!

Oscar Wilde

It is sweet to dance to violins
        When Love and Life are fair:
To dance to flutes, to dance to lutes
        Is delicate and rare:
But it is not sweet with nimble feet
        To dance upon the air!

I Never See the Stars at Night

George Barker

I never see the stars at night
        waltzing round the Moon
without wondering why they dance when
        no one plays a tune.

I hear no fiddles in the air
        or high and heavenly band
but round about they dance, the stars
        for ever hand in hand.

I think that wise ventriloquist
        the Old Man in the Moon
whistles so that only stars
        can hear his magic tune.

Night Song

Frances Cornford

On moony nights the dogs bark shrill
Down the valley and up the hill.

There's one who is angry to behold
The moon so unafraid and cold,
That makes the earth as bright as day,
But yet unhappy, dead, and grey.

Another in his strawy lair,
Says: 'Who's a-howling over there?
By heavens I will stop him soon
From interfering with the moon.'

So back he barks, with throat upthrown;
'You leave our moon, our moon alone.'
And other distant dogs respond
Beyond the fields, beyond, beyond.

POEMS FOR FUN

The Lama

Ogden Nash

The one-l lama,
He's a priest.
The two-l llama,
He's a beast.
And I will bet
A silk pyjama
There isn't any
Three-l lllama.

Tongue-Twisters

Unknown

Betty Botter bought some butter,
     But she said, 'My butter's bitter.
If I put it in my batter,
     It will make my batter bitter.
If I buy some better butter,
     It will make my batter better.'
So she bought some better butter,
     And it made her batter better.

✳ ✳ ✳ ✳

How many cans can a cannibal nibble
     If a cannibal can nibble cans?
As many cans as a cannibal can nibble
     If a cannibal can nibble cans.

I saw Esau sawing wood,
   And Esau saw I saw him;
Though Esau saw I saw him saw
   Still Esau went on sawing.

✳ ✳ ✳ ✳

Theophilus Thistledown, the successful thistle-sifter,
In sifting a sieve of unsifted thistles,
Thrust three thousand thistles
Through the thick of his thumb.
If, then, Theophilus Thistledown, the successful
   thistle-sifter,
In sifting a sieve full of unsifted thistles,
Thrust three thousand thistles
Through the thick of his thumb,
See that thou, in sifting a sieve of unsifted thistles,
Do not get the unsifted thistles stuck in thy thumb.

✳ ✳ ✳ ✳

She sells sea-shells on the sea-shore.
   The shells she sells are sea-shells, I'm sure.
So if she sells sea-shells on the sea-shore,
   Then I'm sure she sells sea-shore shells.

Fleet Flight

Unknown

A flea met a fly in a flue;
Said the flea, 'Let us fly';
Said the fly, 'Let us flee';
So they flew through a flaw in the flue.

Limericks

Unknown

There was a young lady of Ryde,
Who ate some green apples and died.
    The apples fermented
    Inside the lamented,
And made cider inside her inside.

✳ ✳ ✳ ✳

There was a young person from Perth
Who was born on the day of his birth.
    He was married, they say,
    On his wife's wedding day,
And died when he quitted the earth.

✳ ✳ ✳ ✳

A diner while dining at Crewe
Found quite a large mouse in his stew.
    Said the waiter, 'Don't shout
    And wave it about,
Or the rest will be wanting one, too!'

The bottle of perfume that Willie sent
Was highly displeasing to Millicent.
　　　　Her thanks were so cold
　　　　That they quarrelled, I'm told,
Through the silly scent Willie sent Millicent.

There was a young bard of Japan
Who wrote verse that no one could scan;
　　　　When they told him 'twas so,
　　　　He replied, 'Yes, I know,
But I always try to get as many words into the last line
　　　　as I possibly can.'

School Dinners

Unknown

If you stay to school dinners
Better throw them aside;
A lot of kids didn't,
A lot of kids died.
The meat is made of iron,
The spuds are made of steel;
If that don't kill you,
The afters will.

Macavity: The Mystery Cat

T. S. Eliot

Macavity's a Mystery Cat: he's called the Hidden Paw—
For he's the master criminal who can defy the Law.
He's the bafflement of Scotland Yard, the Flying
    Squad's despair:
For when they reach the scene of crime—*Macavity's not
    there!*

Macavity, Macavity, there's no-one like Macavity,
He's broken every human law, he breaks the law of
    gravity.
His powers of levitation would make a fakir stare,
And when you reach the scene of crime—*Macavity's not
    there!*
You may seek him in the basement, you may look up in
    the air—
But I tell you once and once again, *Macavity's not there!*

Macavity's a ginger cat, he's very tall and thin;
You would know him if you saw him, for his eyes are
    sunken in.
His brow is deeply lined with thought, his head is
    highly domed;
His coat is dusty from neglect, his whiskers are
    uncombed.
He sways his head from side to side, with movements
    like a snake;
And when you think he's half asleep, he's always wide
    awake.

Macavity, Macavity, there's no one like Macavity,
For he's a fiend in feline shape, a monster of depravity.
You may meet him in a by-street, you may see him in
    the square—
But when a crime's discovered, then *Macavity's not
    there!*

He's outwardly respectable. (They say he cheats at
      cards.)
And his footprints are not found in any file of Scotland
      Yard's.
And when the larder's looted, or the jewel-case is rifled,
Or when the milk is missing, or another peke's been
      stifled,
Or the greenhouse glass is broken, and the trellis past
      repair—
Ay, there's the wonder of the thing! *Macavity's not
      there!*

And when the Foreign Office find a Treaty's gone
      astray,
Or the Admiralty lose some plans and drawings by the
      way,
There may be a scrap of paper in the hall or on the
      stair—
But it's useless to investigate—*Macavity's not there!*
And when the loss has been disclosed, the Secret
      Service say:
'It *must* have been Macavity!'—but he's a mile away.
You'll be sure to find him resting, or a-licking of his
      thumbs,
Or engaged in doing complicated long division sums.

Macavity, Macavity, there's no-one like Macavity,
There never was a Cat of such deceitfulness and suavity.
He always has an alibi, and one or two to spare:
At whatever time the deed took place—MACAVITY
      WASN'T THERE!
And they say that all the Cats whose wicked deeds are
      widely known
(I might mention Mungojerrie, I might mention
      Griddlebone)
Are nothing more than agents for the Cat who all the
      time
Just controls their operations: the Napoleon of Crime!

The Platypus

Oliver Herford

My child, the duck-billed platypus
A sad example sets for us:
From him we learn how indecision
Of character provokes derision.
This vacillating thing, you see,
Could not decide which he would be,
Fish, flesh or fowl, and chose all three.
The scientists were sorely vexed
To classify him; so perplexed
Their brains, that they, with rage at bay,
Called him a horrid name one day—
A name that baffles, frights and shocks us,
Ornithorhynchus Paradoxus.

Jabberwocky

Lewis Carroll

'Twas brillig, and the slithy toves
Did gyre and gimble in the wabe;
All mimsy were the borogoves,
And the mome raths outgrabe.

'Beware the Jabberwock, my son!
The jaws that bite, the claws that catch!
Beware the Jubjub bird, and shun
The frumious Bandersnatch!'

He took his vorpal sword in hand:
Long time the manxome foe he sought—
So rested he by the Tumtum tree,
And stood awhile in thought.

And as in uffish thought he stood,
The Jabberwock, with eyes of flame,
Came whiffling through the tulgey wood
And burbled as it came!

One, two! One, two! And through and through
The vorpal blade went snicker-snack!
He left it dead, and with its head
He went galumphing back.

'And hast thou slain the Jabberwock?
Come to my arms, my beamish boy!
Ah frabjous day! Callooh callay!'
He chortled in his joy.

'Twas brillig, and the slithy toves
Did gyre and gimble in the wabe;
All mimsy were the borogoves,
And the mome raths outgrabe.

The Heffalumps

Rosemary Marriott

They gorgon on the gridges,
And they bathe in gummy gools,
They raddle round the rolders
With their alabaster stools.
They inhabit carawodgities,
In groups of seven or eight,
And in the sugger seasons,
They attempt to hibernate.
They walk by alliwaddling,
And go for runny trots.
They cultivate gardenias
In alabaster pots.
They rallow with the Rurigines,
And wallow in the wough (wuff),
And muddihydrenate themselves
With slimy gooly stuff.
They eat the lumptious bumberworm
With honey-bottomed bees
And drink the gooly waters
Under harawurly trees.
They greet their friends by horrolling
And make a grooly din.
They scratch their shilly feet
Against their rinkle-ringy skin.
They shelter under hoolah trees
From splurgipuddling rain
And when it is uphottening
They waddle out again.
Their bodies are of greyish hue
With undulating humps,
They're really quite boristical
The rhiny heffalumps.

Caractacus the Crab

A. Roberts (aged 13)

It happened on a boobious day
When I was feeling slightly drab
I chanced to see Caractacus,
    Caractacus the crab.
Caractacus, Caractacus,
Some people think he's crackedacus
(His brain is so compactacus)
    Caractacus the crab.

It happened in the shining dusk
When I wasn't feeling quite so drab
By accident I stepped on him,
    Caractacus the crab,
I fear I broke his bactacus,
I crackedacus Caractacus
(His brain was so compactacus)
And now he's not intactacus,
    Caractacus the crab.

If You Should Meet a Crocodile

Unknown

If you should meet a crocodile,
    Don't take a stick and poke him;
Ignore the welcome in his smile,
    Be careful not to stroke him.
For, as he sleeps upon the Nile,
    He thinner gets and thinner;
And whene'er you meet a crocodile
    He's ready for his dinner.

I Had a Hippopotamus

Patrick Barrington

I had a hippopotamus; I kept him in a shed
And fed him upon vitamins and vegetable bread;
I made him my companion on many cheery walks,
And had his portrait done by a celebrity in chalks.

His charming eccentricities were known on every side,
The creature's popularity was wonderfully wide;
He frolicked with the Rector in a dozen friendly tussles,
Who could not but remark upon his hippopotamuscles.

If he should be afflicted by depression or the dumps,
By hippopotameasles or the hippopotamumps,
I never knew a particle of peace till it was plain
He was hippopotamasticating properly again.

I had a hippopotamus; I loved him as a friend;
But beautiful relationships are bound to have an end;
Time takes, alas! our joys from us and robs us of our
      blisses;
My hippopotamus turned out a hippopotamissis.

My housekeeper regarded him with jaundice in her eye;
She did not want a colony of hippopotami;
She borrowed a machine-gun from her soldier-nephew
      Percy,
And showed my hippopotamus no hippopotamercy.

My house now lacks the glamour that the charming
      creature gave,
The garage where I kept him is as silent as the grave;
No longer he displays among the motor-tyres and
      spanners
His hippopotamastery of hippopotamanners.

No longer now he gambols in the orchards in the
      spring;
No longer do I lead him through the village on a string;

No longer in the mornings does the neighbourhood
        rejoice
To his hippopotamusically-modulated voice.

I had a hippopotamus; but nothing upon earth
Is constant in its happiness or lasting in its mirth;
No joy that life can give me can be strong enough to
        smother
My sorrow for that might-have-been-a-hippopotamother.

An Evening in November

Unknown

'Twas an evening in November,
As I very well remember,
I was strolling down the street in drunken pride,
But my knees were all a-flutter,
So I landed in the gutter,
And a pig came up and lay down by my side.

Yes, I lay there in the gutter,
Thinking thoughts I could not utter,
When a colleen passing by did softly say:
'Ye can tell a man that boozes
By the company he chooses.'
At that the pig got up and walked away!

Henry King

*who chewed bits of string and was early cut off
in dreadful agonies*

Hilaire Belloc

The chief defect of Henry King
Was chewing little bits of string.
At last he swallowed some which tied
Itself in ugly knots inside.
Physicians of the utmost fame
Were called at once; but when they came
They answered, as they took their fees,
'There is no cure for this disease.
Henry will very soon be dead.'
His parents stood about his bed
Lamenting his untimely death,
When Henry, with his latest breath,
Cried—'Oh, my friends, be warned by me,
That breakfast, dinner, lunch and tea
Are all the human frame requires . . .'
With that the wretched child expires.

The Sad Story of a Motor Fan

H. A. Field

Young Ethelred was only three,
Or somewhere thereabouts, when he
Began to show in divers ways
The early stages of the craze
For learning the particulars
Of motor-bikes and motor-cars.
He started with a little book
To enter numbers which he took
And, though his mother often said,
'Now, do be careful, Ethelred;
Oh, dear! Oh, dear! what shall I do
If anything runs over you?'
(Which Ethelred could hardly know,
And sometimes crossly told her so),
It didn't check his zeal a bit,
But rather seemed to foster it;
Indeed it would astonish you
To hear of all the things he knew.
He guessed the make (and got it right)
Of every car that came in sight,
And knew as well its m.p.g.
Its m.p.h. and £.s.d.,
What gears it had, what brakes, and what—
In short he knew an awful lot.

Now, when a boy thinks day and night
Of motor-cars with all his might
He gets affected in the head,
And so it was with Ethelred.
He called himself a 'Packford Eight'
And wore a little number plate
Attached behind with bits of string,

And cranked himself like anything
And buzzed and rumbled ever so
Before he got himself to go.
He went about on all his fours,
And usually, to get indoors,
He pressed a button, then reversed,
And went in slowly, backmost first.
He took long drinks from mug and cup
To fill the radiator up
Before he started out for school
('It kept,' he said, 'his engine cool');
And when he got to school he tried
To park himself all day outside,
At which the Head became irate
And caned him on his number plate.

So week by week he grew more like
A motor-car or motor-bike,
Until one day an oily smell
Hung round him, and he wasn't well.
'That's odd,' he said, 'I wonder what
Has caused the sudden pains I've got.
No motor gets an aching tum
Through taking in petroleum.'
With that he cranked himself, but no,
He couldn't get himself to go,
But merely buzzed a bit inside,
Then gave a faint chug-chug and died.
Now, since his petrol-tank was full,
They labelled him 'Inflammable',
And wisely saw to it that he
Was buried safely out at sea.
So, if at any time your fish
Should taste a trifle oilyish,
You'll know that fish has lately fed
On what remains of Ethelred.

Without Wonder

Unknown

Twinkle, twinkle, little star;
I don't wonder what you are.
You're the cooling down of gases
Forming into solid masses.

Accident

Unknown

An accident happened to my brother Jim
When somebody threw a tomato at him—
Tomatoes are juicy and don't hurt the skin,
But this one was specially packed in a tin.

Home Truths from Abroad
Unknown

'Oh! to be in England
Now that April's there,
And whoever wakes in England
Sees some morning' in despair;
There's a horrible fog i' the heart of the town,
And the greasy pavement is damp and brown;
While the raindrop falls from the laden bough,
In England now!

'And after April when May follows,'
How foolish seem the returning swallows.
Hark! how the east wind sweeps along the street,
And how we give one universal sneeze!
The hapless lambs at thought of mint-sauce bleat,
And ducks are conscious of the coming peas.
Lest you should think the spring is really present,
A biting frost will come to make things pleasant,
And though the reckless flowers begin to blow,
They'd better far have nestled down below;
An English spring sets men and women frowning,
Despite the rhapsodies of Robert Browning.

The Computer's First Christmas Card

Edwin Morgan

```
jollymerry
hollyberry
jollyberry
merryholly
happyjolly
jollyjelly
jellybelly
bellymerry
hollyheppy
jollyMolly
marryJerry
merryHarry
hoppyBarry
heppyJarry
boppyheppy
berryjorry
jorryjelly
moppyjelly
Mollymerry
Jerryjolly
bellyboppy
jorryhoppy
hollymoppy
Barrymerry
Jarryhappy
happyboppy
boppyjolly
jollymerry
merrymerry
merrymerry
merryChris
asmerryasa
Chrismerry
asMERRYCHR
YSANTHEMUM
```

Weather Forecast

Unknown

The rain it raineth every day
        Upon the just and unjust fellow,
But more upon the just, because
        The unjust has the just's umbrella.

Great Fleas

Unknown

Great fleas have little fleas upon their backs to bite 'em,
And little fleas have lesser fleas, and so *ad infinitum*.
The great fleas themselves in turn have greater fleas to
        go on,
While these again have greater still, and greater still,
        and so on.

Today's Most Popular Drink

Michael Thompson (aged 11)

I've drunk the drink of today, today,
I've drunk the drink of today.
I've drunk today's most popular drink;
It turned me green, then turned me pink;
But I've drunk today's most popular drink;
I've drunk the drink of today.

I've drunk the drink that THEY all drink,
I've drunk the drink THEY drink.
It turned me blue, it turned me yellow,
And I heard people say, 'Poor fellow.'
But I've drunk today's most popular drink,
I've drunk the drink of today.

I've drunk today's most popular drink,
But a week in bed with a dreadful pain
Has made me think to think again
Before I drink that drink again,
Today today's most popular drink,
The drink THEY drink,
      Or so I think—
Or shall I think again?

This is Going to Hurt Just a Little Bit

Ogden Nash

One thing I like less than most things is sitting in a dentist
    chair with my mouth wide open,
And that I will never have to do it again is a hope that I am
    against hope hopen.
Because some tortures are physical and some are mental,
But the one that is both is dental.
It is hard to be self-possessed
With your jaw digging into your chest,
So hard to retain your calm
When your fingernails are making serious alterations in your
    life line or love line or some other important line in your
    palm;
So hard to give your usual effect of cheery benignity
When you know your position is one of the two or three in life
    most lacking in dignity.
And your mouth is like a section of road that is being worked
    on,
And it is all cluttered up with stone crushers and concrete
    mixers and drills and steam rollers and there isn't a nerv
    in your head that you aren't being irked on.
Oh, some people are unfortunate enough to be strung up by
    thumbs,
And others have things done to their gums,
And your teeth are supposed to be being polished,
But you have reason to believe they are being demolished,
And the circumstance that adds most to your terror
Is that it's all done with a mirror,
Because the dentist may be a bear, or as the Romans used to say
    only they were referring to a feminine bear when they sa
    it, an ursa,
But all the same how can you be sure when he takes his crow-
    bar in one hand and mirror in the other he won't get mix
    up, the way you do when you try to tie a bow tie with th

aid of a mirror, and forget that left is right and vice versa?
And then at last he says That will be all; but it isn't because he
then coats your mouth from cellar to roof
With something that I suspect is generally used to put a shine
on a horse's hoof,
And you totter to your feet and think, Well it's all over now
and after all it was only this once,
And he says come back in three monce.
And this, O Fate, is I think the most vicious circle that thou
ever sentest,
That Man has to go continually to the dentist to keep his teeth
in good condition when the chief reason he wants his teeth
in good condition is so that he won't have to go to the
dentist.

Hi There, Haiku!

Stuart Wynn Jones

To write a Haiku

You need a pen, some paper

And a high I.Q.

Epitaphs

Unknown

Here lies I and my three daughters
Killed by drinking Cheltenham waters.
If we'd kept to Epsom Salts
We wouldn't be lying in these 'ere vaults.

Here lies John Bun;
He was killed by a gun;
His name was not Bun, but Wood,
But Wood would not rhyme with Gun,
But Bun would.

Here lies what's left
Of Leslie Moore.
No Les
No more.

Here lies the body of Michael Shay
Who died maintaining his right of way.
His case was clear and his will was strong—
But he's as dead as if he'd been wrong.

Here lies the body of Ann Mann
Who lived an old woman
And died an old Mann.

On a Dentist

Stranger! Approach this spot with gravity.
John Brown is filling his last cavity.

Acknowledgements

Thanks are due to the authors (or their executors), their representatives and publishers mentioned in the following list for their kind permission to reproduce copyright material:

George Barker: 'O Child beside the Waterfall' and 'I Never See the Stars at Night' from *To Aylsham Fair* (Faber and Faber Ltd).

Patrick Barrington: 'I Had a Hippopotamus' published in *Punch*.

Andrew Barton Paterson: 'Waltzing Matilda', published by Angus & Robertson Ltd, by permission of Retusa Pty Ltd.

Hilaire Belloc: 'Henry King', 'Matilda' and 'Tarantella' from *Complete Verse* (Gerald Duckworth & Co. Ltd).

Gerard Benson: 'Blue Jeans and Silver Guitars'.

Sidney Carter: 'The Lord of the Dance', Stainer & Bell Ltd.

Charles Causley: 'Timothy Winters' from *Collected Poems* (Macmillan London Ltd), by permission of David Higham Associates Ltd.

Frances Cornford: 'Night Song' from *Collected Poems* (Hutchinson Publishing Group Ltd).

Walter de la Mare: 'The Snowflake', The Literary Trustees of Walter de la Mare and The Society of Authors as their representative.

T. S. Eliot: 'Macavity: The Mystery Cat' from *Old Possum's Book of Practical Cats* (Faber and Faber Ltd).

Richard Kell: 'Pigeons' from *Differences* (Chatto & Windus).

Rudyard Kipling: 'A Smuggler's Song' from *The Definitive Edition of Rudyard Kipling's Verse* (Macmillan London Ltd), by permission of The National Trust for Places of Historic Interest or Natural Beauty.

D. H. Lawrence: 'Spray' from *The Complete Poems of D. H. Lawrence*, Laurence Pollinger Ltd, The Estate of Mrs Frieda Lawrence Ravagli.

Vachel Lindsay: 'Daniel' from *Collected Poems* (Macmillan Publishing Company), © renewed 1948 by Elizabeth C. Lindsay.

John Masefield: from 'Reynard the Fox', the Society of Authors as the literary representative of the Estate of John Masefield.

Edwin Morgan: 'The Computer's First Christmas Card'.

J. B. Morton: 'The Dancing Cabman' from *The Best of Beachcomber*. (William Heinemann Ltd), by permission of A. D. Peters & Co. Ltd).

Index of titles

Index of poets